So wird es gemacht:

Öffne das mini LÜK®-Kontrollgerät und lege die Plättchen in den unbedruckten Deckel! Jetzt kannst du auf den Plättchen und im Geräteboden die Zahlen 1 bis 24 sehen.

Beispiel: Seite 2
An English Breakfast
Nimm das Plättchen 1 und lies Satz 1: Mr. Charles Cheeser is an .... Welches der beiden Wörter fehlt an dieser Stelle?
Englishman mit der Zahl 12.
Die 12 ist auch die Feldzahl im Kontrollgerät, auf die du das Plättchen legen mußt. Lege also das Plättchen 1 auf das Feld 12 im Geräteboden! Die Zahl **1** muß nach oben zeigen.

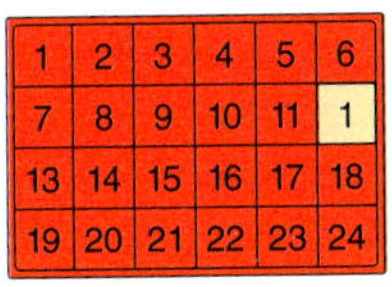

So mußt du weiterarbeiten, bis alle Plättchen im Geräteboden liegen. Schließe dann das Gerät und drehe es um! Öffne es von der Rückseite!

Wenn du das bei der Übungsreihe abgebildete Kontrollmuster siehst, hast du alle Aufgaben richtig gelöst.

Passen einige Plättchen nicht in das Muster, dann hast du dort Fehler gemacht. Drehe diese Plättchen da, wo sie liegen, um, schließe das Gerät, drehe es um und öffne es wieder! Jetzt kannst du sehen, welche Aufgaben du falsch gelöst hast.

Nimm diese Plättchen heraus und suche die richtigen Ergebnisse! Kontrolliere dann noch einmal! Stimmt jetzt das Muster?

Das System ist für alle Übungen gleich: Die roten Aufgabennummern im Heft entsprechen immer den LÜK-Plättchen aus dem Kontrollgerät. Die Zahlen hinter den Lösungen sagen dir, auf welche Felder im Kontrollgerät du die Plättchen legen mußt.

Und nun viel Spaß!

Dieses Papier wurde aus chlorfrei gebleichtem Zellstoff hergestellt

An English Breakfast

1	Mr. Charles Cheeser is an ____________.	egg 2 Englishman 12
2	He is also a cook at the ____________.	street 13 Swanson Hotel 9
3	He has got a ____________ and his name is Albert.	record 17 son 7
4	Albert's cousin from New York is ____________ him.	sitting 21 visiting 11
5	His cousin's ____________ is Freddy, little Freddy.	boy 16 name 1
6	Little Freddy's father is a ____________ in New York.	funny 6 cook 10
7	He is a fat man, so people call him ________ Freddy.	small 23 fat 21
8	Little Freddy is also fat, so people call ________ little fat Freddy.	he 12 him 5
9	Charles Cheeser must ____________ to work early, so he can't make breakfast.	sleep 19 go 8
10	It's six o'clock in the morning and Charles is talking to Albert about ____________.	train 18 breakfast 2
11	"Now, Albert, ____________ want you to make little fat Freddy a typical English breakfast.	Charles 14 I 6
12	All the things you need are in the ____________."	fridge 22 bed 10

13 Albert ____________ the fridge. — blue 1 / opens 23

14 "Dad, what can we ____________?" — work 7 / drink 3

15 Mr. Cheeser says, "There are ____________ for orange juice. — apples 9 / oranges 19

16 And you can make some ____________." — banana 3 / tea 24

17 "Great, Dad, and I can make some hot porridge with ____________. — open 22 / milk 15

18 And then we can have some toast with __________." — marmalade 20 / plane 4

19 "Fine, son, and you can make some bacon and ____. — eggs 16 / elbows 24

20 And please give little fat Freddy some biscuits with ____________. — sand 11 / butter 18

21 I must go to ____________ now, goodbye son." — work 14 / find 5

22 "Goodbye, Dad." Albert can hear the alarm clock ____________. — walking 22 / ringing 4

23 Now Albert is making breakfast, and he hears little fat Freddy walk into the ______________. — kitchen 17 / colour 8

24 Little fat Freddy smiles and says, "Look, I ________ some wonderful pizza and cola for breakfast!" — has 15 / have 13

Marcy

That's Marcy Stanley sitting on her new [1] __________. She is the [2] __________ girl in my class. Her hair is [3] ________________ long and she is pretty.

new 21	bike 19	very 24

I [4] __________ Marcy, but I'm afraid to tell her. Look, [5] __________ is smiling at me. [6] __________ can't I tell her I like her?

Why 22	like 8	she 5

Marcy [7] ___________ onto her bike. She is still looking at [8] ___________. Marcy is [9] ___________ watching where she is going.

not 11	climbs 15	me 13

She falls [10] ___________ onto the road. Oh no! A [11] ___________ is coming. It is driving very [12] ___________.

down 18	bus 2	fast 16

The bus driver 13 __________ see Marcy. I must 14 __________ Marcy.

I 15 __________ over and carry her away from the bus.

run 23	doesn't 7	help 9

Then I pull her bike off the 16 _________. "Marcy, Marcy are 17 _______ O.K?"

Marcy smiles at me with her 18 ___________ blue eyes.

you 3	pretty 12	road 20

19 _________ she falls into my arms. But Marcy doesn't 20 _________.

She 21 _________ me on the lips.

kisses 17	Then 4	speak 1

But then I hear a 22 __________. "Wake up, Billy, 23 ___________.

Billy, you are having a 24 _________!"

voice 10	dream 6	wake up 14

Wilma's Violin

1	"George, what is ______	17 know, Thelma."
2	"I don't ______	4 her violin."
3	"Well, she must practise ______	13 Wilma doing?"
4	Mrs. Winfield goes ______	3 her daughter talking.
5	She hears ______	6 the phone with Carol.
6	Wilma is talking on ______	2 upstairs.
7	Mrs. Winfield knocks ______	5 on Wilma's door.
8	Then she opens the ______	15 it's my mother.
9	"Wait a second, Carol, ______	1 door and walks in.
10	Yes, Mum, what ______	14 practise your violin now!"
11	"Wilma, you must ______	16 is it?"
12	"Oh Mum, I want to watch ______	18 the Davis Cup tennis match on TV."

13 "I'm sorry, Wilma, ______________

14 Mrs. Winfield ______________

15 "Carol, what can ______________

11 goes downstairs.

9 I do?

7 you must practise now!"

16 I want to watch tennis, ______________

17 "Wilma, I have an easy answer to ______________

18 You can play some violin ______________

23 your question.

22 music on your CD player.

20 but Mum says I must practise on my violin."

19 Then you can put on your ______________

20 "Oh, that's ______________

21 Wilma puts a CD with violin ______________

21 music into her CD player.

12 headphones and watch TV."

19 a great idea, Carol."

22 Then she puts on her headphones and ______________

23 Mrs. Winfield says, "Listen, George, our ______________

24 "Yes, you're right Thelma, and she is ______________

24 switches on the TV.

8 daughter is playing her violin."

10 such a good violin player!"

Mrs. Gossip

1	Oak Street is a wonderful place to ______________.	live 12 great 3
2	Nobody locks their ______________ on Oak Street.	tables 10 doors 4
3	Mrs. Gossip ______________ at 9 Oak Street.	lives 7 van 19
4	The Bensons live ______________ at 10 Oak Street.	next door 11 door 13
5	Look, the Benson family is coming out of their ______________ now.	sponge 24 house 19
6	Mrs. Gossip ______________ her window.	opens 3 asks 22
7	Then she says, "______________, Mr. and Mrs. Benson.	Good morning 15 Good night 7
8	______________ are you going this morning?"	How many 8 Where 23
9	Mrs. Gossip must ______________ everything about everybody.	idea 2 know 8
10	"Good morning, Mrs. Gossip. We are going ______________."	shopping 20 red 17
11	Mr. and Mrs. Benson get into their car and ________.	next door 5 drive off 24
12	A few minutes later a furniture van stops ___________ the Bensons' house.	in front of 16 new 1

13 Four big ______________ get out of the furniture van.
vegetables 20
men 5

14 One man has got a piece of paper and he is wearing ______________.
tomatoes 21
sun-glasses 9

15 The men go into the Bensons' house and carry out a ______________.
sofa 1
black 12

16 Mrs. Gossip sees the men and says, "Oh, gangsters!". And she calls the ________________.
police 6
telephone book 14

17 "Hello, this is the Maple Street police station. ______ is speaking?"
What 4
Who 22

18 "My ______________ is Mrs. Gossip and gangsters are next door at 10 Oak Street."
address 16
name 2

19 "Mrs. Gossip, don't worry. A police car is _________ at once."
coming 21
fast 18

20 A police car stops ______________ the furniture van.
behind 18
a garden 6

21 A policeman sees the men and says, "Stop, ________ are you doing?"
when 11
what 14

22 The man with the sun-glasses takes out a piece of paper and then he puts on his reading ___________.
glasses 10
cup 9

23 "It's right here officer. We must take the ___________ from 100 Oak Street to Hamptonville."
furniture 17
garden 23

24 The policeman answers, "Please ______ your glasses all the time, sir. This is 10 Oak Street, not 100 Oak Street!"
see 16
wear 13

Randy's Front Tooth

Little Randy's front [1] __________ hurts. Wilma sees her brother with his fingers in his [2] __________. She asks, "[3] __________ the matter, Randy?"

What's 22	tooth 7	mouth 23

"Oh Wilma, my front tooth is [4] __________. I can push it with my [5] __________, but I can't get it out." Wilma says, " I've got [6] __________ idea.

tongue 16	loose 20	an 12

Let's [7] __________ it out. I can pull it out with my [8] __________. No, wait Randy. I have a [9] __________ idea.

pull 17	better 21	fingers 1

Go into your room and get [10] __________ string." Randy gets the [11] __________. "O.K., Randy, tie the string around your [12] __________ tooth."

front 6	some 15	string 14

Randy 13 ________ the string around his front tooth. Then Wilma ties the string 14 ________ Randy's doorknob. "No, Wilma, please stop. I'm 15 ________."

afraid 10	around 11	ties 19

"O.K., Randy, 16 ________ got a better idea." Wilma unties the string and 17 ________ walk into Randy's room. Wilma opens the 18 ________.

I've 8	window 9	they 5

"Randy, give me a big 19 ________." She takes a 20 ________ book and ties the string around the book. "Wait, Wilma! Stop! I don't 21 ________ your idea."

like 3	big 13	book 18

Randy 22 ________ out of his room and into the kitchen. Then he gets an apple and he 23 ________ into it. Randy is 24 ________ now. "Look, Wilma!" Randy's tooth is in the apple.

smiling 4	bites 2	goes 24

The Birthday Party (Part One)

1	My name ______________ Donna Ashley.	are 12 is 21
2	It is my birthday and my mother wants me to ______________ a birthday party.	have 13 work 20
3	She wants the ______________ to play lots of games.	children 18 mother 24
4	And she ______________ us to sing, too.	wants 22 plays 11
5	But I don't ______________ to play or sing.	cake 4 want 6
6	I have a good ______________.	happy 23 idea 14
7	I can ______________ my Uncle Waldo to come to my party.	eat 15 ask 2
8	Uncle Waldo ______________ for the circus.	works 10 work 18
9	He ______________ a fire-eater and his circus friends say "hot lips" Waldo to him.	am 21 is 17
10	I call Uncle Waldo on the ______________.	piano 1 telephone 5

11 He says he ____________ come over to my party.
can 9
comes 22

12 He also says he can bring a ____________.
clown 1
want to 10

13 And he can bring a group of dancing ____________.
dogs 16
wants to 2

14 My mother thinks our birthday circus is a good ____________.
idea 20
table 16

15 But my mother is afraid of a fire in the ____________.
house 24
water 17

16 She says, "I don't want Uncle Waldo to start a ____________ in our house!"
dining-room 5
fire 15

17 "Oh Mum, Uncle Waldo is very ____________."
careful 7
clown 19

18 Then she says, "I know I ____________ careful, but I don't know if Uncle Waldo is careful."
are 13
am 23

19 "Please, Mum, I can put a bucket of ____________ in the room."
fire 6
water 8

20 "O.K., Donna, but please tell your ____________ to be careful."
Uncle 3
birthday 14

21 It is now three o'clock and my birthday guests are in our ____________.
dining-room 11
fridge 9

22 We carry out the dining-room ____________ and chairs.
table 19
guests 3

23 And then all the guests sit down on the ____________.
sing 8
floor 4

24 Now my birthday "circus" can ____________.
drink 7
begin 12

The Birthday Party (Part Two)

1	First the dogs dance to some ______________.	music 3 chairs 6
2	Everyone laughs when they __________ to rap music.	want 23 dance 17
3	Then the clown walks into the room on his ________.	music 19 hands 14
4	He has got a red ______________ and is very funny.	fire 10 nose 4
5	Then Uncle Waldo walks into the dining-room with a ______________.	stick 20 street 17
6	He takes out a ______________.	fire-brigade 15 match 18
7	Now one end of the stick is ______________.	burning 24 going 18
8	Suddenly Uncle Waldo puts the stick into his ______________.	suddenly 3 mouth 10
9	Then "hot lips" pulls ______________ the stick.	matchbox 21 out 13
10	The fire is out and everyone is ______________.	happy 19 wonderful 12
11	We clap our hands and Uncle Waldo says, "I'm ______________."	thirsty 9 yoghurt 4
12	My mother gives him a ______________.	glass of water 23 glass table 5
13	After that, my mum and Uncle Waldo go into the ______________.	yoghurt 7 kitchen 16
14	Mum wants to get my birthday ______________.	cake 6 water 11

15 She asks Uncle Waldo for his ____________.

fire-eater 13
matchbox 2

16 Now the ____________ on the cake are burning.

candles 15
circus 1

17 One of the candles ____________ down.

falls 11
listens 8

18 It falls onto the kitchen ____________.

chair 1
book 16

19 A ____________ is on the chair.

pretty 2
newspaper 12

20 Oh no! There is ____________.

plastic 24
smoke 21

21 The newspaper is ____________.

burning 7
sleeping 11

22 My mother is ____________, "Fire! Fire!"

playing 6
shouting 5

23 Uncle Waldo quickly throws his ____________ on the burning newspaper.

water 22
clown 9

24 Then Uncle Waldo says, "You must be ____________ with fire."

kitchen 22
careful 8

The Race

1 The 1,000 metres race ________	7 best runner from Waddleton.
2 Mark Hardy is the ________	22 but he looks unhappy.
3 He walks over to Mary Wills, ________	11 begins in five minutes.
4 "Mary, I'm ill, you ________	8 win the race, Mary."
5 "But Mark, you know I ________	12 must run the race for me."
6 "I know you can ________	15 am a 100 metre runner."
7 "But Mark, Bonzo Sludge is ________	1 running in the 1,000 metres.
8 He's the best ________	21 he's good, but he's not."
9 "Don't worry, Mary. He only says ________	5 runner from Oxbridge."
10 Bonzo Sludge walks ________	6 must run for me."
11 Mark says, "Hey Bonzo, I'm ill, so Mary ________	16 over to them.
12 Bonzo laughs, "Ha, ha, a ________	2 girl, she can't win."

13 Then Bonzo says, "Girls ____________

14 And then a voice says, "The ________

15 Mary's face is red. She looks at Mark ____________________

16 Everyone is waiting, ____________

17 The boys and girls from Oxbridge ____________________

18 Now Bonzo is in front of ________

19 Bonzo turns and looks at the boys and girls, ______________

20 But just then, Mary ____________

21 Mary is the ______________

22 The boys and girls from ____________

23 Bonzo sees Mary, but now ________

24 Mary says, "Bad luck, Bonzo, but you ____________________

9 and says, "Don't worry, I can run for you."

23 can wash clothes, but they can't run."

19 1,000 metres race begins in two minutes."

13 are shouting, Bonzo! Bonzo!

10 Mary, with only 20 metres to go.

24 but then the race begins.

3 winner, not Bonzo!

17 runs past Bonzo.

14 then he holds up his arms and also shouts, Bonzo! Bonzo!

18 he is red in the face.

20 Waddleton are all happy.

4 can always wash my socks."

Our Maths Teacher

1 Mr. Frumpet is our maths ______________.

book 15
teacher 17

2 He often ______________ a lot of things.

forgets 1
arrives 8

3 He says, "Oh, excuse me boys and ______________.

girls 10
headphones 2

4 I ______________ have my maths book.

yes 2
don't 6

5 Can I have your ______________ book today, Charles?"

very 12
maths 3

6 Or he says, " I don't have my glasses, can you ______________, Diana?"

think 11
read 14

7 Or, "I don't have my lunch today, can I have a ______________ please?"

sandwich 7
nose 21

8 Mr. Frumpet ______________ asks us silly questions.

please 6
also 23

9 When he asks silly ______________, we give him silly answers.

questions 9
nobody 5

10 Here he comes ______________.

now 4
only 17

11 "Good ______________, boys and girls.

morning 12
tomatoes 24

12 I have a maths ______________ for you.

lunch 10
problem 20

13 A cat can drink three ________ of milk in one hour. — cups 5 / oranges 13

14 How many cups of milk can it drink in five ________? — hours 13 / stairs 14

15 Jimmy, do you know the ________?" — question 3 / answer 21

16 "Mr. Frumpet, I don't ________ a cat is thirsty after three cups of milk." — think 18 / drink 7

17 "________, that's not the answer. — Then 4 / No 19

18 Janet, what about ________?" — me 1 / you 22

19 "I don't know, Mr. Frumpet. I don't have a ________." — cat 8 / television 23

20 Mr. Frumpet is getting very ________ now. — angry 11 / wonderful 20

21 He says, "If we can't ________ in class, then I must give you homework. — wait 9 / work 15

22 Boys and girls do ________ 15, 16, 17, 18 and 19." — exercises 2 / stop 16

23 But we don't ________ about homework. — think 18 / worry 24

24 You see, the next ________, Mr. Frumpet always forgets we have homework. — day 16 / door 19

Babysitting for Willy

Mr. and Mrs. Winfield must go out, but their babysitter is [1] ____________.

"Oh dear, Thelma," Mr. Winfield says, "[2] __________ are we going to do?" "Well, George, I think our [3] ____________ can babysit for us."

What 13	daughter 18	ill 4

"Yes, but Wilma is only eleven years [4] __________." "We don't have time to find [5] ___________ babysitter, George!" "O.K., I [6] ___________ ask her."

can 14	old 3	another 23

"Wilma, Wilma can you come here [7] ___________?" Wilma comes down the [8] ____________. Mr. Winfried asks, "Wilma, can you please babysit for your little [9] ____________?"

please 19	brother 17	stairs 10

"Oh Dad, I want [10] _________ play with Carol." "Well, Carol can come to our [11] __________." "O.K., Dad, but little Willy doesn't [12] __________ Carol."

like 20	to 24	house 9

"Well, Willy can play in his [13] __________." Mr. and Mrs. Winfield leave the house and Carol [14] __________. Carol and Wilma [15] __________ up the stairs with little Willy.

arrives 1	room 16	walk 5

Wilma says, "Now, Willy, go into [16] __________ room and play." "I don't want to go into [17] __________ room, Wilma!" "Go and draw a [18] __________ or write your name.

your 15	picture 6	my 7

And here is some [19] __________, now please go." "O.K., Wilma, I [20] __________ chocolate." Carol and Wilma go into Wilma's room and watch [21] __________.

television 11	chocolate 8	love 22

The chocolate is now all over Willy's [22] __________. "Now, I can draw a picture and write my [23] __________." Oh no, look! Willy is writing his name on the [24] __________ with his chocolate fingers.

wall 12	name 21	fingers 2

Word List in Alphabetical Order

A

a / an	ein, eine
about	
– what about …?	wie ist es mit …?
address	Adresse
afraid	Angst haben, sich fürchten
– afraid of	Angst haben vor
after	nach
after that	danach
alarm clock	Wecker
all	alle
– all over	überall
– all the time	die ganze Zeit
also	auch
always	immer
am (to be)	bin (sein)
angry	böse, wütend
another	noch ein
answer	Anwort
to answer	antworten
apple	Apfel
are (to be)	sind (sein)
around	um, herum
to arrive	ankommen
to ask	fragen

B

to babysit – babysitting	Kinder hüten
bacon	Speck
bad luck	Pech
to be	sein
be careful	sei vorsichtig
to begin	anfangen
behind	hinter
best	der, die, das beste
better	besser
big	groß
bike	Fahrrad
birthday	Geburtstag
biscuit	Keks
to bite	beißen
black	schwarz
blue	blau
book	Buch
breakfast	Frühstück
to bring	bringen, mitbringen
brother	Bruder
bucket	Eimer
to burn – burning	brennen
bus driver	Busfahrer
but	aber

C

to call (on the telephone),	anrufen, telefonieren
– to call him "hot lips"	er wird "hot lips" genannt
can	können
can't	nicht können
candle	Kerze
careful	vorsichtig
to carry	tragen
– to carry away	wegtragen
– to carry out	hinaustragen
children	Kinder
chocolate	Schokolade
circus	Zirkus
to clap our hands	Beifallklatschen
to climb	klettern
clothes	Kleidung
clown	Clown
colour	Farbe
to come – coming	kommen
– to come down	herunterkommen
– come on	komm schon
– to come over	vorbeikommen
cook	Koch
cousin	Cousin, Vetter

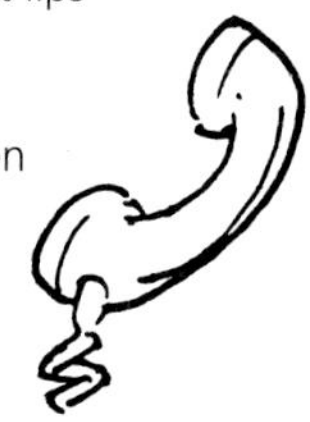

D

dad	Vater
to dance – dancing	tanzen
daughter	Tochter
day	Tag
oh dear	oje
dining-room	Eßzimmer
to do	tun
doesn't	nicht tun
doorknob	Türknauf
down	unten, herunter
downstairs	unten (im Haus)
to draw	zeichnen
dream	Traum
to drink	trinken
to drive	fahren
to drive off	wegfahren

E

early	früh
easy	einfach
to eat	essen

elbows	Ellenbogen
end	Ende
Englishman	Engländer
everybody	jeder
everyone	jeder
everything	alles
excuse me	Entschuldigung, Verzeihung
exercises	Übungen

F

face	Gesicht
to fall	fallen
– to fall down	herunterfallen
– to fall onto	fallen auf
fast	schnell
fat	dick, fett
few	wenig
to find	finden
fine	in Ordnung, gut
fire	Feuer
fire-brigade	Feuerwehr
fire-eater	Feuerschlucker
first	zuerst, erste (r, s)
five	fünf
floor	Fußboden
for	für
to forget	vergessen
fridge	Kühlschrank
friend	Freund
from	aus / von
front tooth	Schneidezahn
funny	lustig
furniture	Möbel

G

game	Spiel
gangster	Verbrecher, Ein-
garden	Garten
to get – getting	holen, kriegen
– to get into	einsteigen
– to get out	herauskommen, aussteigen
to give	geben
glasses	Brille
– reading glasses	Lesebrille
– sun-glasses	Sonnenbrille
a glass of water	ein Glas Wasser
glass table	Glastisch
to go – going	gehen
– to go out	weggehen, ausgehen
good	gut
goodbye	auf Wiedersehen
good morning	Guten Morgen
good night	Gute Nacht
great	großartig, prima
group	Gruppe
guest	Gast

H

happy (un-)	glücklich (unglücklich)
has (to have)	hat (haben)
– has got	hat
he	er
headphones	Kopfhörer
to hear	hören
to help	helfen
her	ihr
here	hier
him	ihm, ihn
his	sein
to hold	halten
– to hold up	hochhalten
homework	Hausaufgaben
hot	heiß
hour	Stunde
how many	wie viele
hurt	verletzen

I

I	ich
idea	Idee
if	ob, wenn, falls
ill	krank
in	in
– in front of	vor
– into	hinein
is (to be)	ist (sein)
it	es

J

juice	Saft
just then	gerade in dem Augenblick

K

to kiss	küssen
to knock	klopfen
to know	kennen, wissen

L

later	später
to laugh	lachen
to leave	verlassen
let's (to let)	laßt uns … (lassen)
to like	mögen
to listen	zuhören
to live	wohnen, leben
to lock	schließen
to look	schauen
– to look at	anschauen

loose	locker
lots of	viel
to love	lieben, mögen
lunch	Mittagessen

M

to make	machen
man / men	Mann / Männer
match	Streichholz
matchbox	Streichholzschachtel
maths	Mathe(matik)
maths problem	Rechenaufgabe
me	mich, mir
minute	Minute
mouth	Mund
mum	Mutti
must	müssen
mustn't	müssen nicht, dürfen nicht
my	mein, meine

N

name	Name
to need	brauchen
new	neu
newspaper	Zeitung
next	nächst
– the next day	am nächsten Tag
– next door	nebenan
no	nein
nobody	niemand
not	nicht
now	jetzt, nun
– now, Willy	nun Willy

O

o'clock	Uhr
officer	Polizeibeamter
often	oft
old	alt
only	nur
opens (to open)	öffnet (öffnen)
our	unser, unsere
out	aus / heraus

P

people	Leute
piano	Klavier
piece of paper	Blatt Papier
place	Platz, Ort
plastic	Plastik
to play – playing	spielen
please	bitte
police	Polizei
policeman	Polizist
police station	Polizeirevier
porridge	Haferbrei
to practise	üben
pretty	hübsch
to pull	ziehen
– to pull out	herausziehen
to push	schieben
to put	stellen
– to put on	aufsetzten, anziehen

Q

question	Frage
quickly	schnell

R

race	Rennen
to read	lesen
reading glasses	Lesebrille
record	Schallplatte
red	rot
right	richtig
– you're right	du hast recht
to ring – ringing	klingeln, läuten
road	Straße
room	Zimmer
to run – running	laufen
– to run past	vorbeilaufen
runner	Läufer

S

sand	Sand
sandwich	belegtes Brot
to say	sagen
second	Sekunde
– wait a second	Augenblick bitte
to see	sehen
she	sie
shopping	Einkaufen
to shout – shouting	rufen, schreien
silly	albern
to sit – sitting	sitzen
– to sit down	sich setzen
to sleep – sleeping	schlafen
small	klein
to smile – smiling	lächeln
smoke	Rauch
socks	Socken
some	einige, irgendwelche (r, s)
something	etwas
son	Sohn
to speak – speaking	sprechen
sponge	Schwamm
stairs	Treppe,Treppenstufen
to start	anfangen, starten
stick	Stock